Sherry
Remember to
Keep the SON in your

May Holt

Jer 29:11

Every Single Day

Devotionals That Speak to Single Adults

Max Holt

Turning Point Communications, Inc.
Franklin, TN

Every Single Day:
*Devotionals That Speak
To Single Adults*

Published by
Turning Point Communications, Inc.

Unless otherwise noted, all Scripture quotations in this book are taken from Kings James version of the Bible (Public Domain). All italics and use of bold lettering used in Scripture quotations are added by the author.

All rights reserved. No part of this publication may be reproduced, stored in retrieval system, or transmitted, in any form or by any means, electronic, mechanical, photocopying, recording, or any other except for brief quotation in printed reviews or articles, without the prior written permission of author.

Cover Design by Alan Corry

ISBN 1-59306-002-5

Printed in the United States of America

Copyright © 2003 by Max Holt

For more information, please contact
Turning Point Communications, Inc.
P.O. Box 681982
Franklin, TN 37068

FORWARD

When we think about someone writing a devotional, we develop a mental picture of a story being told - tied to a Biblical principal - that is designed to make us think about our current relationship with God. Now, there are hundreds of good devotionals written every year; but few actually focus on the issues that face single adults in today's world. In this, his first book, Max Holt has done a great job of telling just these kind of stories. By using his own brand of humor and telling about real life situations, we begin to reflect on our own relationship with God and how we relate to others. A lot of the stories come from his own personal life experience - either as a boy living on a Texas farm, as a veteran of the US Army or as a pastor working with single adults. As we read through each devotional, we begin to think about our own life - past and present. The Common Sense Application section of each devotion is designed to get us thinking about practical things we can do; and we are challenged to take actions that can have a very positive impact on our future.

One of the things that Max believes about people is the importance of their character. If you build your character, then you will earn the respect of those around you. It is also important to know single adults have to become content and learn to deal with their singleness before they will be ready for a marriage relationship. Max addresses the practical issues of living a life of integrity as a Christian single. He also gives practical insight into successful relationships.

I have known Max Holt for nearly eight of his nine years in

single adult ministry. We have served on leadership teams and taught at many of the same conferences. Max has a great personality and loves to tell jokes - but I must warn you, sometime his jokes are a little corny! As you get to know Max, you will learn he is proud of his farm boy heritage. As a young man, he began a career in the US Military, serving 22 years - starting out as a Private, earning his wings in Fight School, and retiring as a Army Lieutenant Colonel. He then began his second career serving our Lord in ministry. Although he admits that he did not start out in ministry to work with single adults, he has grown to love this ministry with a passion. I have seen how God has used him to reach hundreds of single adults at his local church in Clarksville, TN. Max has also helped train hundreds of single adult leaders throughout the country and even internationally as he leads workshops and seminars on single adult ministry. Max Holt loves the Lord, loves his family, and he loves his ministry calling - working with single adults.

The publishing process has been exciting; and I am proud to be working with Max to put this material in your hands. I believe you will enjoy reading these devotionals; and if you actually put into practice some of his Common Sense Applications, you will find your relationship with God growing and your relationship with others developing into stronger more meaningful friendships. You might even find yourself telling some of Max's stories to your friends as illustrations for life's journey.

Alan Corry
President / Founder
Turning Point Communications, Inc.

DEDICATION

This work is dedicated to my wife, Sandy, my best friend and the most important person in my life. It was her vision in the middle of the night that confirmed the idea God had given me to write such a book for Single Adults. She inspired me to begin putting into words my experiences and those that Single Adults have shared with me over the years.

I also dedicate it to the single adults of S.P.L.A.S.H. (Single People Loving And Serving Him), which is the Single Adult Ministry of Hilldale Baptist Church in Clarksville, Tennessee. They are the ones who taught me a sensitivity and understanding of the issues Single People deal with Every Single Day of their lives.

Special thanks goes to Cathy Rau, a former member of S.P.L.A.S.H., who did the editing for this work.

Max Holt

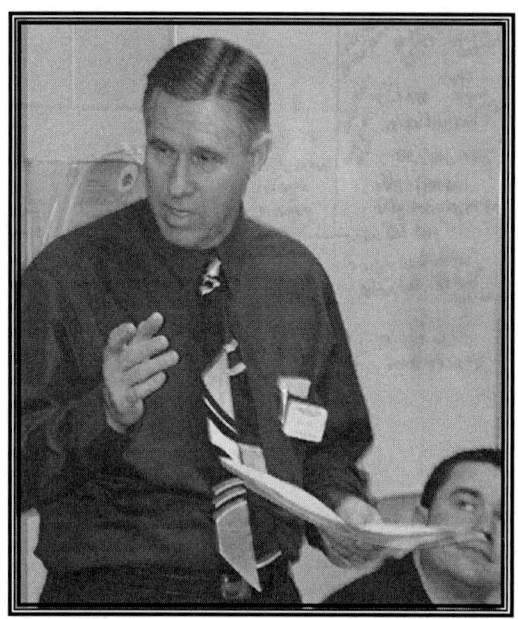

Max Holt encouraging a Sunday Morning Bible Study at Hilldale Baptist Church in Clarksville, TN.

Max enjoys talking with friends.

INTRODUCTION

Every Single Day single adults live in a challenging world; a world that often encourages mediocre choices in life and seldom extols the benefits of excellence. Single Adults are just like married adults; they want and need encouragement and to find purpose in their lives. Although I am a VMP (Very Married Person) having been married for 36 years, thousands of single adults throughout my career have been teaching me what it is like to be single in a world, especially the church, that seems to cater mainly to married couples. Their counsel has helped me to focus on the issues they most often face.

There are many devotional books available in virtually every bookstore in the country, both Christian and secular stores. Few of those books, however, are targeted at the lives and needs of Single Adults. Most devotional books make no effort to lead the reader through to the application of the devotional thought offered. This book is an attempt to bridge the gap between understanding the spiritual and life principles involved and applying those principles to daily life. My hope is that the reader will actually put into practice the Common Sense Application recommended for each devotion and revisit these devotionals from time to time to determine the results.

Max

A BRAND NEW YEAR

Happy new year!
Gluckliches neues Jahr! (German)
Seh-heh yea bouk mahn-he-baht uo-seh-yoo! (Korean)
C HoBbim Toaom (Russian)
Felice Anno Nuovo! (Italian)
Feliz Ano Nuevo! (Spanish)

Any way you say it, the hope is still the same for all of us. The new year brings an opportunity to forget last year with all its challenges and missed possibilities. It is an opportunity for Single Adults to look forward to the excitement of 365 days in which to make changes and grow in all areas of their lives. Most of us make some sort of resolutions or promises to ourselves about things we are going to stop or start during the new year. As we all know, it is easy to make promises but it takes determination, patience, time and honesty to keep most of them.

Suppose every promise you made, I mean every one, was written down and you were required to sign on the dotted line? You would probably think twice before making most of them. It is amazing how we sometimes flippantly agree to do or go or say something, only to forget and say, "Oh, well, I'll just say I'm sorry and everything will be okay." The problem is that the person to whom you made the promise may begin to reevaluate your honesty and friendship. If you have had the problem of failing to keep promises, I encourage you to put that habit behind you and start fresh with the four things mentioned above: determination, patience, time and honesty. Philippians 3:13-14 says, "Brethren, I count not myself to have apprehended: but this one thing I do, forgetting those things which are behind, and reaching forth unto those things which are before, I press toward the mark for the prize of the high calling of God in Christ Jesus" Imagine that; there is a prize for forgetting the old things and pressing forward toward the new things!

COMMON SENSE APPLICATION

1. Carry a small note pad for a week and write down every promise of any kind that you make. Record the time and date you made good on each promise. You will be surprised what you discover.

2. Ask a close trusted friend to tell you truthfully if you have ever broken a promise to them. If so, ask forgiveness and keep the promise if possible. Promise not to break future promises!

3. Ask God to grow you into a consistent promise keeper. You will be amazed how your reputation will improve among all those around you.

PERSONAL NOTES

PICK UP STICKS

*Sometimes the smallest things in life
turn out to be the most significant.*

The Swallows of San Juan Capistrano are a flock of birds that resides in San Juan Capistrano, California. Each year they migrate to South America and stay the winter in Argentina. The route to Argentina is about 12,000 miles long and takes 30 days for the swallows to complete. For hundreds of years a legend circulated that the swallows migrated to the Holy Lands (www.hrh.servsite.com/danapoint/hist2.htm). As the story goes, the swallows, which can only fly distances of several hundred miles without rest, would cross the ocean by carrying twigs in their beaks and at some point over a calm part of the ocean they would drop their small sticks and land on them to rest! After resting, they would supposedly leave the sticks behind and continue to their destination. The story may be a legend but it illustrates an important principle of spiritual survival.

God always provides a way for us to survive. He wants us to grasp the reality of Jesus' death on the cross and to understand that we must hold on to it if we are to survive for eternity. I have discovered that in a world with challenges as rough as an ocean, the Old Rugged Cross will float quite nicely. I pray that you will get a grip on it daily and rest. Romans 8:38-39 says, "For I am persuaded, that neither death, nor life, nor angels, nor principalities, nor powers, nor things present, nor things to come, Nor height, nor depth, nor any other creature, shall be able to separate us from the love of God, which is in Christ Jesus our Lord."

COMMON SENSE APPLICATION

1. In the legend, the swallows survived with what they took with them. You will survive the same way. Begin by writing on small cards any scripture verses, prayer reminders, inspirational quotes or spiritual goals on which you want to concentrate. Place some around the house in easily seen locations as reminders of what to think about. Take some to work with you and read them during breaks or lunch. Change the cards as often as necessary to keep fresh ideas and spiritual goals in your mind. If your situation permits, take your Bible everyday and visit with God through His Word.

2. Take more good spiritual stuff with you by committing yourself to grow as a Christian in every area of your life.

3. Arrange to meet with Christian friends during breaks or lunch whenever possible for the purpose of encouraging and teaching each other; take the good stuff back to work with you.

PERSONAL NOTES

ONLY THE LONELY

*Loneliness has nothing to do with location;
it is a state of mind.*

Loneliness is one of the most frequent complaints I hear from Single People, especially the formerly married, whether divorced or widowed. The complaint comes more often from those who no longer have children at home requiring their care or affording some companionship. However, all Single People experience loneliness from time to time. God made mankind in His image to have fellowship with Him. It is natural to see how we, as weak humans, need earthly fellowship even more. Just as infants need love, touch and nurturing to properly develop, we also need interaction with others to feel important and loved.

Relationships do not have to be romantic, sexual or physical in order to be significant. Single Adults who want to honor God in their relationships will find ways to allow their day-to-day professional relationships and Christian friendships to fulfill their needs for companionship. Just being with someone will not necessarily remove loneliness. I've seen Single People who felt alone in a crowd and I've also seen married people who were lonely in their marriages. The real key to combating loneliness starts with your attitude. If you find reasons to feel sorry for yourself and tag yourself with the label lonely then you will feel that way.

The Bible says this; "But seek ye first the kingdom of God, and his righteousness; and all these things shall be added unto you" Matthew 6:33. So, if you want one of the "given to you" things to be a feeling of love and significance then do something about it; take action!

COMMON SENSE APPLICATION

1. Work on building a closer relationship with God. (Remember the seek first part?)

2. Join a local Christian Single Adult Group and seek out the serious Christians in the group as your friends. Spend time with them.

3. Within a Christian group, seek out a ministry team which focuses on meeting specific needs in peoples' lives, then get involved.

4. Join a local Big Brother Big Sister organization.

5. Volunteer to drive a Meals On Wheels route.

6. Take food to, or volunteer to sit with, a sick friend or shut-in.

7. Join an organization that majors in helping others.

8. Remember, you may be the only Jesus someone else will ever see.

PERSONAL NOTES

FIRE WARNING!

*The only thing worse than not getting a warning
is treating all warnings as though they were false.*

As the pilot of a comfortable twin-engine airplane in the Republic of Vietnam I pretty much had it made, at least while in the air. We flew at altitudes that were usually safe from enemy fire. One day, while flying at 9,000 feet over the mountains, I was already bored with the routine flight. My copilot was a single guy named Dave. He and I often joked about the old saying, "Flying is hours and hours of boredom, punctuated by moments of stark terror." Just as I finished my first cup of coffee our moment of terror happened; the Fire Warning Alarm sounded! Startled is not a strong enough word to describe our reaction in the cockpit. The loud warning horn and the flashing red lights indicated a fire in the left engine. The temperature gage and a visual check of the engine through the window showed no signs of a fire but there was too much at stake to ignore the warning. Dave switched the radar transponder to the emergency position while I radioed the situation to the radar controller and requested emergency landing at the nearest airfield. As it turned out, the warning system had failed due to a bad wire and there was no actual fire in the engine. Regardless, I did the right thing. You can't take chances when lives are at stake!

I often encounter Single People who take all kinds of risks in their lives, even when the warnings are very evident. Statistics indicate that divorce rates are higher for 2nd, 3rd and 4th marriages, yet many divorced people jump into another marriage before they've even begun to heal from the previous one. My counseling has shown that the highest divorce rate is among those who live together before marriage, yet many Single Adults think they will be an exception to the statistics, only to crash and burn in their relationships. Some will use immoral or illegal methods to get ahead in their careers, only to be discovered and lose the reputation they spent years building. I admire Single Adults who heed warning signs in their lives and take action to ensure their safety. I appreciate their use of good spiritual judgment by listening to God's warning system and deciding to ask Him for guidance. We find in Matthew 24:42, Acts 21:3-4, 1 Timothy 4:1-6 and Jude 3-4 different warnings God gave to His people to help protect them. What He gave then, applies now!

COMMON SENSE APPLICATION

When faced with an inner warning that you are in violation of God's will for your life you should:

1. Pray, spend more quality time with God and listen to His guidance.

2. Ask a trusted Christian friend to be your accountability partner to help you analyze the warning sign you are receiving.

3. Recommit yourself to see and hear the warnings God places in your life.

4. Use the good spiritual common sense God gave you to run from temptation!

5. When you do heed the warning sign, and survive, thank God for His goodness and share your success with someone else who is struggling or who needs encouragement.

BROKEN PIECES

*When a marriage breaks apart,
children are pieces of the brokenness.*

For years my wife was an elementary school nurse at one of the six elementary schools in our area. Many of the children who came to see her shared the details of their home life. A large percentage of them came from single parent homes, mostly due to divorce, and some of them lived under conditions that would sadden all of us.

One day, a small child came into the clinic with a stomachache, a common complaint of school children. When attempting to make contact with the father listed in the records the child stated, "Don't call him, he's not my dad anymore, he moved out." The sad truth is, many fathers, and mothers, believe they can just walk away from the responsibilities of marriage, parenting and sometimes even the responsibilities of life. This child and many like him, suffer from the uncertainties and fears created by the decisions of their parents. The realization that children are some of the pieces of a broken marriage serves to remind us that children suffer the most when divorce happens. Too many people take lightly the decisions they make about relationships.

In today's society, the media and even some friends often encourage us to *watch out for No. 1*. They say, "If it feels good, do it." But all actions and decisions have consequences that sometimes last a lifetime. I often counsel single parents whose children are still suffering even ten years following a divorce. I realize that in many cases there was nothing that could have been done to prevent a divorce. However, many give up too soon in trying to resolve conflicts in their marriages or they wait too long to address issues that became major ones because they were allowed to build too large. When you enter into a marriage contract with someone please remember, if children are a part of the family you have an increased responsibility that God expects you to honor; to take care of helpless children. When divorce is chosen the children must be made to feel as safe and secure as possible and you must *never* use them as *pawns* or *message bearers* between parents. Jesus said in Matthew 18: 5 - 6, "And whoso shall receive one such little child in my name receiveth me. But whoso shall offend one of these little ones which believe in me, it were better for him that a millstone were hanged about his neck, and that he were drowned in the depth of the sea."

COMMON SENSE APPLICATION

1. If you have gone through a divorce, regardless of how long ago, find a Divorce Recovery program at a local church and attend. You'll be surprised how it will help you!

2. If you have children from a previous marriage, attend a Single Parenting Workshop. If you are not the custodial parent, attend anyway; it will help with custody and visitation issues.

3. If you are considering remarriage, remember, the children will always be more affected than you think. *Do not* get married until you and your intended have gone through premarital counseling and have fully addressed the blended family issues you will face.

PERSONAL NOTES

ELECTRONIC RELATIONSHIPS

*"Hello, you've reached the home of Jennifer, and Nicole,
we're not home right now, so, leave a message
and we'll call you right back ... we promise!"
(BEEEEEEEP)*

*"Hi, Nicole, this is Matt,
I'm returning your call on my machine where you
answered the message I left on your machine yesterday,
or was it the day before? Anyway, I left it in answer to your
message from Saturday, or was it Friday, . . ."*

Relationships are awkward enough when we encounter people face to face; when you put electronic devices between us, it gets worse. Answering machines are nothing more than barriers we can selectively put up and take down to fit the situation. Sure, answering machines serve a vital function in our fast-paced society but we humans tend to overdo just about every thing good in our lives. We have Caller ID, Caller ID Blocker, Caller ID Blocker Identifiers, Voice Mail, Beepers, e-mail, PDAs, Answering Services, etc. I am in an e-mail group with a bunch of Army buddies who can sometimes get a little *testy* with each other over certain issues. I reminded them one day that it was too easy to see the other person as just *lines of characters on a computer screen* rather than a real person with needs and feelings.

How do you see Single Adults or others in your life? As a voice on an answering machine tape, e-mail characters from cyberspace, or a real person with whom you can communicate and get to know? I heard of one single man who used an answering machine message to break up with his girlfriend. How tacky can you get!?

I've heard several speakers say that over 90 percent of all Single Adults want to be married at some point in their future. It would be great if those who want to marry would understand that significant relationships require *work* (effort), *time* and an atmosphere free from barriers to communication and interaction. In Hebrews 10:25 the words, "Not forsaking the assembling of ourselves together, as the manner of some...," does not just apply to church worship services but is an encouragement to *get together* often as Christians so that we can form bonds of friendship and relationships of significance as brothers and sisters in Christ. It is during these times that permanent relationships can form, face to face!

COMMON SENSE APPLICATION

1. Turn off your answering machine when you are home and talk to whoever calls, salesmen and all. Hint: If one of those telemarketers calls, say, "Let me make you a deal, I'll listen to your sales pitch if you'll listen to mine." Have a 30-second version of your testimony, when you accepted Christ, ready and share it with them. Recommend to them that they call local churches in their area to find one that ministers to people in their category; single, married, etc.

2. When leaving messages on other answering machines leave just the minimum essentials and tell them when to call so they can speak to you in person for full details.

3. You can use answering machines creatively by doing something like this: Buy one of those *large* bags of pre-popped popcorn, call everybody in your friendship group and leave a message for them to bring a large soft drink and meet you somewhere (a park maybe) for a great time and a chance to meet some new *colonels (kernels!)*! You get the idea! Have fun.

THE RACE TO THE TOP

In your effort to climb to the top in life it would be a good idea to make sure you're on the right hill.

My brother Dan, child number five out of ten kids, was always a leader; he was very competitive. One day near a neighboring farm he and the neighbor's teenager challenged each other to a tree-climbing race. The goal was to be the first to climb to the top of a skinny thirty-foot pine tree growing near their house. They readied themselves at the base of the tree, one on either side. The go signal was given and I watched them start the race up through the limbs. Since they were obscured by the branches as they climbed, we weren't sure who was winning but we soon became sure of something else; their combined weight was more than the top of that skinny tree could support. We heard a loud crack and watched the top five feet of that tree, along with both climbers, come crashing through the other limbs and land on the ground, with Dan on the bottom! The rest of us jumped to untangle limbs and boys. Dan was the most seriously injured with scrapes, scratches and torn clothing. The worse part was his face; it was all bloody, his nose was broken and he was almost unconscious. I remember how frantically our mother arrived on the scene and finally got Dan to the doctor sixteen miles away. Dan and the neighbor should have planned their climb more carefully. Without a plan, they picked the wrong tree to climb. Today Dan still bears the scars of that fall.

Are you racing through life, trying to climb to the top without a plan? Have you stopped and analyzed your life enough to know if you're even on the right hill? Have you written down your dream based on what you feel God has called you to do? Do you have a plan of action on how you want to succeed and what to do when you achieve success? What part does God play in your career plans? Have you prayed and asked God's direction for your life?

You have probably heard the words, "Stop and smell the roses." Many Single Adults are rushing through their lives so fast they don't even know there are roses. Psalm 46:10 says, "Be still, and know that I am God: I will be exalted among the heathen, I will be exalted in the earth." It is during those being still times that you can know God's Calling in your life. When you slow down enough to listen to your Heavenly Father and exalt Him in your life you will have a much better chance of arriving at the top of the right hill and having a plan on how to stay there longer.

COMMON SENSE APPLICATION

1. Read the book, "Calling," by Frank Tillapaugh and Richard Hurst, Dreamtime Publishing. Contact them at www.dreamtime2.com or call toll free (888) 603-7326.

2. Pray for an understanding of God's Calling in your life.

3. Write down your goals and time frames for pursuing the Call.

4. Make an assessment at least quarterly on how well you are climbing toward your Call.

5. Make a commitment to change directions when you determine you are climbing the wrong way.

PERSONAL NOTES

THE DEVIL MADE ME DO IT

My family background was bad,
I was diaper trained too late,
I was born too early,
I was born too late,
my parents hated me too much,
my parents loved me too much,
I wasn't given enough attention,
I was spoiled,
I wasn't lucky,
. . . and so on!

The devil made me do it, was a phrase made famous by the great comedian, Flip Wilson. The phrase was funny when he said it but it takes on all too much reality in our world today. Many of the excuses above are used by Single People to blame their failures or actions on someone else. In the book "How Could You Do That?!", Laura Schlessinger deals with the issue of victimization; the tendency to cast blame outside yourself for your weaknesses. She said, "Call me a heretic, but I believe that even with bad stuff in your past, you have choices. Everyone must overcome something. That simply, is life. Acknowledging that you are responsible for messing up your own life gives you the power to change things."

In his INJOY Life Club leadership tape "Winning Is An Inside Job," John Maxwell quoted some research done with prisoners at a major prison. The researcher tried to determine exactly what led to these inmates committing their crimes. Every prisoner claimed to be innocent, to have been framed. The researcher determined that he could not find a larger group of innocent people anywhere! These prisoners could not bring themselves to admit their failures. Admitting fault is the first step toward turning your life around.

Would you like to change something about your life? Taking responsibility for your part in being where you are now can help you confess faults to the ultimate change agent, Jesus Christ. A relationship with Him begins with confession. 1 John 1:9 says, "If we confess our sins, he is faithful and just to forgive us our sins, and to cleanse us from all unrighteousness." Admitting your shortcomings can clear the way for you to move your life forward in a new direction.

Common Sense Application

1. Title a blank piece of paper, "Personal Life." Confess in writing those sins or weaknesses that seem to be hurting your life, relationships, finances, habits, etc. Take responsibility for those things and ask God to help make the changes necessary.

2. Title a second page, "Career." List the bad choices, lack of skill, lack of effort and sin associated with limiting your career. Ask God to forgive the sin and make a commitment to improve the quality of your work. Make plans to acquire the experience and training necessary to move forward in your career.

3. Title a third page, "Spiritual Relationship." List those things, sins and weaknesses that seem to distance you from God. Confess that only He can restore you to full fellowship with Him and ask Him to do that. Deal honestly with the spiritual issues between you and God and between you and others.

4. Keep track of the progress in all three areas and celebrate victories with a trusted friend.

STOP HORSING AROUND IN THE PAST

In the rodeo of life, when you discover your horse is dead, dismount and get a new horse!

One warm afternoon on our small northeast Texas farm my brother Frank and I were playing rodeo by riding our stick horses around the house. During a water break we passed our mother's sewing machine and noticed a large, full spool of white thread mounted on the spindle, ready for use. Mom made most of our clothes and used a lot of thread. As Frank reached to get the thread there were several questions that should have entered our minds, but didn't, such as, can we play with it (no), is it the last one (it was), will we get in trouble (yes!), and what will be the consequences (I don't like to think about it!). Frank took the spool and slid it over the nail that held the rains on his horse, then tied the loose end to the corner post of the front porch. We both began running with our trusty steeds between our legs and watched the white thread begin to unwind from the spool onto the ground along side the house. We had made three trips around the house and as we approached the front porch again the thread ran out, leaving the spool spinning on the nail. We stopped and watched the spool spin, realizing that our original decision was not as good as we first thought. We jumped off the horses and began trying to rewind the thread onto the spool. After one circle around the house the partially rewound thread was dirty, filled with twigs and already twice the size of the original spool! As we rounded the front porch there stood mom, with a small peach tree switch in her hand! As she pulled Frank across her knees in the rocker on the porch he began to cry. I cried too, knowing I was next. Frank said, "I'm sorry, Mom, I'll fix it, I'll clean it up!" That's when our mother lifted him onto her lap and said, "You can't fix it, Frank, we'll have to get a new one!"

I learned that day there are some things in life that you must be very careful with because they can't be fixed. Your heart can never really be fixed like it was before it got broken in a failed relationship. Your reputation can suffer irreparable damage when you deviate from the truth and are discovered. But, when you suffer because of your sin and then reconcile with God, start working to put it behind you. Some things can't be fixed, you just have to start over. Praise the Lord we have a God who majors on new beginnings! The Bible says in Psalm 103:11-12, "For as the heaven is high above the earth, so great is his mercy toward them that fear him. As far as the east is from the west, so far hath he removed our transgressions from us." God is faithful to forgive and to give us a fresh start. So, whatever dead horse you insist upon trying to ride from the past, get off and let God give you a new one! Submit yourself to His leadership and He will keep you riding in style.

COMMON SENSE APPLICATION

1. As you concentrate on moving forward out of the failures of the past, read II Corinthians 5:17 every day for a month. Write it on a business card and take it with you to read during the day.

2. Really let the old things begin to pass away, as the verse states. Be faithful to replace the old things with some new things of God.

3. Ask a trusted Christian friend to be your monitor, to remind you when your conversation and attitudes tend to center too much on the old things.

GET A GRIP

*When you get to the end of your rope,
get a grip and hang on!*

It is the same for all of them, birds, hawks, owls, eagles, chickens and even turkeys. It's a genetic thing. In a discussion with a Veterinarian friend of mine I learned that these winged creatures all have tendons that run from their bodies, down their legs, through their knees, to their feet and finally out into each toe or claw. This unique design allows them to do something that other animals just can't accomplish; it allows them to roost, that is, to sleep while perched on a small surface such as a limb or a narrow board in a chicken coop. How do they do it? When these birds squat or settle down to sleep, they bend their knees. The tendons running through their knees are stretched causing the whole tendon to pull, thus retracting their claws and feet, resulting in a firm grip on the limb or board. With this automatic grip they can sleep peacefully without fear of falling.

The process of bending knees to get a grip provides a great lesson for us. I have observed several areas in which Single Adults need to get a grip, meaning to understand or face reality. First, get a grip on who you are as a Christian. Have you ever really accepted Jesus as your Savior in accordance with Romans 10:10, "For with the heart man believeth unto righteousness; and with the mouth confession is made unto salvation"? If you have, what is it in your life that expresses your salvation? Matthew 7:20 says "Wherefore by their fruits ye shall know them." What spiritual fruits do others see in your life?

Second, get a grip on your attitude. How you see life will determine how you live life. There aren't too many things worse than a person with a bad attitude. Philippians 2:5 says "Let this mind be in you, which was also in Christ Jesus". Does your attitude reflect the mind of Christ?

Third, get a grip on your priorities. All of us decide where, when and how we are going to spend our time, money and our efforts. Unfortunately, many Single Adults let people or cir-cumstances control their priorities. Too many people just drift with life, never deciding what is most important to them and never really accomplishing much toward their growth as a person or in their career. Some of you are near or have past mid-life and still have not made an assessment of where you're going. If you have no target, or goal, you don't know what to shoot at!

COMMON SENSE APPLICATION

1. Reread the salvation scriptures to ensure you understand the process God established by which we become Christians. I like the Roman Road; Romans 3:23, 6:23, 5:8, 10:9-10 and 13, and I John 5:11-13. If you have never truly accepted Jesus as Savior and you are serious about wanting a right relationship with God, do so right now. Pray to Him, confess your sin and ask for forgiveness, ask Jesus to come into your heart and be your Savior, thank Him for saving you and then ask Him to help you make Him Lord, controller, of your life.

2. Ask a close Christian friend to give you an honest monthly attitude check. Listen to yourself as you interact with others. Ask God to help you change your attitude to a positive one.

3. Nothing helps establish priorities better than writing down your daily requirements, deciding what is most important and assigning priority numbers to them. Once established, stick to your priorities.

4. Finally, pray every day!

THE CHECKLIST

When all else fails, read the instructions!

During my first combat tour in Vietnam, I was assigned as a pilot to fly small twin-engine airplanes delivering supplies and passengers all over the country. The airplanes we flew had retractable landing gear and would carry 10 passengers at about 200 miles per hour. One fear every pilot of such an airplane had was to accidentally land gear up, forgetting to put the wheels down. We often kidded about the old saying, "There are only two types of retractable gear pilots: those who have landed gear up and those who are going to!" To prevent such accidents, every pilot is provided a thorough Checklist that outlines in great detail the proper procedures for virtually every action you can take while operating the airplane.

One day one of our flight crews approached a small rugged airfield for landing. It was barely big enough for that size airplane and had just a dirt surface covered by interlocked steel planks to provide a landing strip. It was a dangerous runway that required a lot of planning, a lot of caution and skilled piloting to safely land there. To complicate matters, they were flying in and out of small rain showers, avoiding fighter jets in the area and having to coordinate by radio with three different air traffic controllers at the same time. Needless to say, they were busy and their attention to detail was somewhat strained. Normally, when the power was reduced for landing and the wheels weren't down yet, a loud horn would sound to warn the pilot. But as they made their final approach to the runway they kept the engine power higher, due to turbulence, so the warning never sounded. When both propellers began hitting the runway they realized the wheels weren't down! It was too late. As they listened to the sound of paint and radio antennas being scraped off the belly of the airplane they stopped being pilots and became observers, unable to affect the outcome.

The Landing Checklist became a useless piece of paper. No one got a scratch but that one-quarter-million dollar airplane never flew again.

How often do you get so distracted that you forget the basic things that are most important in your life? Sometimes prayer becomes less frequent, Bible study and worship take a back seat, Christian fellowship and activities become rare and you become an observer rather than a participant in the quality Christian lifestyle God has for you. The Bible is God's Checklist for us, giving us detailed instructions on how to avoid crashing and burning in this complicated world. Psalm 119:9-11 says, "Wherewithal shall a young man cleanse his way? By taking heed thereto according to thy word. With my whole heart have I sought thee: O let me not wander from thy commandments. Thy word have I hid in mine heart, that I might not sin against thee" Use the checklist!

COMMON SENSE APPLICATION

1. Get a Bible with a good concordance and dictionary. Use it to research God's instructions in subject areas affecting your life daily.

2. Ask a leader at your church to help you develop a plan to read the Bible through in the most helpful order.

3. Find and attend, or start, a good Bible Study for your age group; one which is a serious study group, not an eating fellowship.

4. FOLLOW GOD'S CHECKLIST! Happy landings!

BE LIKE MAMA

*When you're in trouble and facing trauma,
call 1-800-YOURMAMA.*

One day on the farm my brother Frank and I and our little sister Connie, ages 8, 6 and 5 respectively, were returning to the house at noon for dinner (that's lunch to you city folks) and found our path to the back door blocked by our mean red-headed rooster we called Tom. He was guarding all the chickens in the yard. We were afraid because previous encounters left us with peck marks and scratches from the sharp talons on his feet.

We tried to sneak around the chickens but each time Tom would move over to challenge us. He would raise his wings, bristle his head feathers and lunge at us. Connie began to cry, afraid we would never get to the house. Frank came up with a great plan (he's famous for great plans!) The plan was for me and him to run past Tom and around the house so Tom would chase us, then Connie would run into the house and tell Mama, who would come outside and rescue us. Great plan! Just as we expected, Tom ran after us as we disappeared around the house. Just as planned, Connie ran into the house. But, she forgot to tell Mama about Tom! We were on our third trip around the house, with Tom gaining on us, when we realized we were in trouble. We were thirsty, hot, tired and losing steam. We began to yell, "Mama, Mama!" She heard us during the fourth circle and as we rounded the back of the house there stood Mama, hiding at the corner with her broom over her shoulder like Babe Ruth. When Tom appeared, Mama hit a home run! Tom became a frequent flyer and feathers went everywhere as he flew about 20 feet backwards! The chickens all gathered around clucking and squawking as Tom staggered off to the hen house. From that day forward Tom ran every time he saw Mama or a broom!

I want to use this event to illustrate four types of Single Adults I often see in my ministry. The first type is like Connie; shallow in their commitments and prone to take lightly the promises they make to you. The second type is like Frank and me; running from their fears and challenges with no real plan on what to do if things don't go right. The third type is like Tom; arrogant, aggressive, insensitive to others, and always demanding their own way. And the fourth is like Mama; a person of integrity, a friend who can be depended on to help you face adversity with confidence and action! Which one are you, Connie, Frank and me, Tom, or Mama, the person of action? Colossians 3:23 says, "And whatsoever ye do, do it heartily, as to the Lord, and not unto men:". I encourage you to be a person of quality and action, just like Mama.

COMMON SENSE APPLICATION

1. Never promise what you can't deliver! If necessary, write down your promises and check the list often to ensure you fulfill them.

2. Stop running from those things that challenge and frighten you. Make a commitment to tackle the hardest tasks first each day and the rest of the day will be a breeze.

3. If you are arrogant and insensitive like Tom you will be the last to realize it. Hints include, the lack of close friends, business associates who avoid you and continuous shallow relationships. Pray, and then ask someone you trust to give you an honest assessment of your personality and listen to him.

4. When you find changes are needed in your life, take action! Make the changes! Be a person of character and action, just like Mama.

DEAR SANTA

Clarksville, TN Newspaper, "The Leaf Chronicle," *Letters To Santa* - December 8, 1996.

Dear Santa,

This is what I want for Christmas. I want freedom. That's right, no toys. I want kids to stop drugs. I want gangs to close down. I want the wars to stop. I want the world to be one big country so we can understand each other. I want more schools. I want the men to go to church. I even want taxes to be lowered. That is what I want for Christmas. I want people to give poor people money. I mean a lot.

Your American,
Justin (7 years old)

Young Justin is certainly an unusual 7 year old. I'm not sure what influenced him to forego the standard fare of toys for Christmas but you can imagine all kinds of challenges he and his friends faced in their community. Whatever those were, they were significant enough to refocus his childish desires on adult issues and enabled him to ask something for others rather than himself.

We can learn from Justin. When was the last time you prayed on behalf of others, without asking something for yourself? All too often we pray generic prayers that mention the world, the sick, the missionaries or the food and then jump right into a long request for our own needs. God cares about us and wants us to cast every care upon Him but He also wants us to have a vision for others. James 5:16 says, "Confess your faults one to another, and pray one for another, that ye may be healed. The effectual fervent prayer of a righteous man availeth much." Did you notice the part where it says we should pray for others so that we may be healed? Our prayers for others do have an impact on us!

COMMON SENSE APPLICATION

1. Make a list of the Christian friends, and non-Christian friends, you interact with.

2. By each friend's name, begin listing the prayer needs that you discover in their lives.

3. Begin to pray specifically for those needs daily and note when you sense God moving in that area of that friend's life.

4. When you feel it is appropriate, let them know you are praying for them and ask them to pray for your specific needs.

PERSONAL NOTES

STOP, STOP, STOP!

*Before you go and start something
it is a good idea to remember
that it's always easier
to start most things
than it is to stop!*

Years ago while working for the Navy in Norfolk, Virginia I went on a tour of the aircraft carrier USS John F. Kennedy. Aircraft carriers are massive ships that dwarf almost anything around. This ship was about 10 stories tall above the water and has about forty feet under water when fully loaded. I was amazed to discover that it is over one thousand feet long, longer than three football fields. Below deck in the aircraft hangar it is completely hollow from end to end, meaning you could have three football games and not interfere with each other. It weighs millions of pounds when fully loaded with all equipment, supplies and 6,000 sailors, a population larger than many towns. Its four nuclear-powered, house-sized propellers can push it across the ocean at speeds exceeding 40 miles per hour! However, our tour guide told us that at full speed, it takes over four miles to stop that ship!

The term used for the force that keeps something moving in the same direction after it has started is the word inertia. The word momentum is similar, meaning that it gets easier to keep moving. As we go through life it is unavoidable that we will collect unneeded stuff that tends to weigh us down, giving us unwanted momentum in the wrong direction. The result is that we have great difficulty making needed changes in our lives.

A good example of being weighed down is when you move. Due to my military career, and now the ministry, we have moved 21 times! I know first hand the hassles of having too much stuff. When you collect stuff that doesn't belong in your emotional, physical, or spiritual life you will find that it takes great effort, sacrifice or even pain to make positive changes. The Apostle Paul wrote about this problem in Hebrews 12:1 where he said, "Wherefore seeing we also are compassed about with so great a cloud of witnesses, let us lay aside every weight, and the sin which doth so easily beset us, and let us run with patience the race that is set before us." It could be that you are so loaded down with stuff that doesn't belong in your life that you are having trouble running your race. Maybe it is time to do some spiritual and lifestyle house cleaning and carry a few loads to the dump!

COMMON SENSE APPLICATION

1. Be honest with yourself, as only you can be, and begin to make an assessment of everything you've included in your life.

2. Write down all the negatives, the things that don't belong in a Christian's life or things that prevent you from attaining your spiritual, relationship and career goals.

3. Beside each negative write down the steps you must take to remove it or change it. Check off each step as you complete it.

4. Pray for God to help you stick to the list until you succeed and when you do, give Him the glory!

THE FROZEN DUCK

*If you are designed to fly, to soar above the earth,
it's dumb to hang around on the ground!*

I remember the words my dad said, "He just stayed too long." He was referring to one of our ducks when we were living on our northeast Texas farm. It was one of those strange winter weather days, when a 'Norther' (cold north wind) moves in and changes 40-degree sunny weather into 25 degree freezing rain in the space of a few minutes. My brothers and I were doing the evening chores in the barn when the freezing weather hit so we hurried all the animals into their respective places and then scattered our flock of ducks, hoping they would fly from the barnyard to their roosting shed a hundred yards away. All of them did except one. He was perched on the top board of the fence and refused to leave, even though the freezing rain was covering his feathers and his feet. We soon gave up on him and all hurried out of the cold and into the house.

The next morning it was about 20 degrees and the ground was covered with a half inch of solid ice. Chores still had to be done so we bundled up and followed dad on the crunchy slippery trip to the barn. As we approached the gate we noticed that our duck was still on that fence, with his feet frozen solid to it! There were feathers lying all around on the ground and he was flapping his wings frantically, trying to fly away. With the duck pecking at him, my brother Dan took his pocketknife and began chipping the ice away. Finally released, and with a large chunk of ice still attached, the duck took off, only to crash into the ground after a few feet. He slid across the yard totally out of control. We finally picked him up, removed the remaining ice and carried him to his roosting shed.

Dad was right, he stayed too long in a place where he did not belong and under conditions unsuitable for ducks. I know many

Christian Single Adults who make a habit of living their lives in places they don't belong and under circumstances inconsistent with God's expectations. Sometimes they have become ingrained in lifestyle habits that can only be broken with great effort and even pain, much like the ice. When looking in the Bible for instruction about relationships with worldly things and people you can find these words in 2 Corinthians 6:17, "Wherefore come out from among them, and be ye separate, saith the Lord. . .". Certainly, you have to form relationships with non-Christians if you intend to influence them with the good things of God, but you can do that without going where you don't belong and doing what violates God's principles. After all, there are some places and situations in which ducks and Christians just do not belong!

COMMON SENSE APPLICATION

1. Take a close look at the lifestyle environment you have developed for yourself. List those places, people and habits which are inconsistent with God's best for your life.

2. Pray and ask God to help you with courage and wisdom as you begin to change those things.

3. Confide in a Christian friend the changes you are trying to make and ask that person to be an accountability partner to monitor progress and help you stay on track.

4. Make a list of quality things and people you can substitute for the inappropriate ones.

5. Promise God and yourself that you're going to rise to the next level of quality in your life.

PLEASE DON'T DIE

What the caterpillar calls the end,
God calls a butterfly.

It was a shocking scene. There was blood everywhere, on the carpet, on the steps and tracked up the walkway. The evidence seemed to confirm that someone had died a violent death. As I surveyed the site I felt uncomfortable and out of place. No one deserved the fate the victim must have suffered. The fact that a Single Adult had died made me take even more notice. I read the report that summarized the tragic death of the innocent.

"Then the soldiers of the governor took Jesus into the common hall, and gathered unto him the whole band of soldiers. And they stripped him, and put on him a scarlet robe. And when they had platted a crown of thorns, they put it upon his head, and a reed in his right hand: and they bowed the knee before him, and mocked him, saying, Hail, King of the Jews! And they spit upon him, and took the reed, and smote him on the head. And after that they had mocked him, they took the robe off from him, and put his own raiment on him, and led him away to crucify him." (Matthew 27: 27-31)

I looked back at the set that had been the scenery for our church's annual Passion Play. Our Easter portrayal of the life, death, burial and resurrection of Christ had left a permanent impact on all who witnessed it and all of us who participated. I admired all the single men and women in our church who helped make it a life-changing experience. But the Single Adult who really touched me was Jesus, as I was reminded that He died for every other Single Adult who would ever be born. He died so that you might live for Him. As I picked up my hammer and joined the others in dismantling the Upper Room, Golgotha and the Tomb, I recommitted myself to live for Him more than I've ever done before.

I see Single Adults often who choose to die a little in many areas of their lives. Their choices cause their relationship with God to die a little, they allow their hope and excitement for life to die a little, they choose a career that is expedient rather than what they really want to do in life and their enthusiasm and professionalism die a little. In John 10:10 Jesus said, "The thief cometh not, but for to steal, and to kill, and to destroy: I am come that they might have life, and that they might have it more abundantly." Jesus died for us that we might have eternal life. He came that we might have life right now to the fullest! So, choose life to the fullest; please don't die!

COMMON SENSE APPLICATION

1. Start now to rekindle your relationship with God by reading His Word and frequent prayer.

2. Analyze your life, including your habits, to identify ruts you may be in and start making the quality choices that will prevent you from dying a little in the ruts of life. Remember, a rut is just a grave with both ends knocked out of it.

PERSONAL NOTES

PROBLEMS OR SOLUTION

*When facing challenges in your life, you are
either part of the problem or part of the solution.*

There are only two kinds of Single Adults in the world, thermometers and thermostats. I meet both types everyday. Thermometers are the ones who are always checking the atmosphere and surroundings in your life, always knowing and telling you how things are, at least according to their perspective. These people do a lot of prying and talking and pretty much keep things stirred up most of the time. They are very judgmental and are quick to cast blame in every direction except theirs. I call them thermometers because they offer no solutions, only reminders of how uncomfortable things are. They complain about their situation but do nothing positive to make changes. They are all talk and no action. Philippians 2:14 has some advice for thermometers, "Do all things without murmuring and disputing:"

Thermostats, on the other hand, are change agents. They not only make an accurate assessment of how things are, they also do what is required to change the situation. You need to be like this and these are the kinds of single friends you need. They can be depended upon to do what is right when they know what the facts are. Thermostats are consistent and dependable. II Thessalonians 3:13 says, "But ye, brethren, be not weary in well doing." This kind of Single Adult will be there for you in good times and bad.

So, I encourage you to test the atmosphere in which you live. Be a thermostat and bring back into proper range those things that are out of adjustment. Also, remember that even thermostats need to be re-calibrated back to the standard every so often. Your standard must always be the Bible.

COMMON SENSE APPLICATION

1. The next time someone complains to you about something affecting them, ask them several questions:

   a. When you prayed about this what did God reveal that you should do? If they haven't prayed about it, stop right then and ask them to pray about it with you.

   b. What action are you going to take because of this problem?

   c. Would you like me to go with you to talk with the person with whom you have a problem? If they say yes then go, but pray beforehand that God will guide your conversation.

2. Be honest with yourself (ask a trusted friend to help you be honest) and determine if you are a thermometer or a thermostat. Ask God to help you transition from the negatives of the first to the positives of the second.

PERSONAL NOTES

DUST TO DUST

You might be a single man...
... if your definition of dust is,
"A protective coating for furniture."

Most single guys are not known for their squeaky-clean, dust free apartments. Somehow men just don't see dusting as a high priority, compared to Monday Night Football and exercising their thumbs on the remote control. It's like the old saying, "Out of sight, out of mind." If they don't look closely, it's out of sight and then they don't mind! After awhile the dust just looks like part of the furniture; sometimes it even matches. When they buy new stuff they look for those dust-colored fabrics.

Finally, though, someone whose opinion matters comes over and convinces (shames) them that it is time to dust. When you watch or help a single man clean his place you'll notice that they have very few nick-knacks. Why? Did you ever try to dust all the nooks and crannies of those little things? Cleaning some single guys' apartments is such a challenging job that they can put it on their resume! One of the biggest problems when a guy cleans his apartment after an extended period of dust collecting is the cost of renting that big trash container! Besides, if you wash dishes too often you might break one. Also, you just kind of miss that familiar smell that says, "You're home!" Honestly, you do feel better when the place finally gets cleaned up. As a matter of fact, guys brag for weeks about how they slaved to get their place clean!

Here are a few questions for both you guys and ladies. How is your spiritual furniture? How are all those things that make up who you are spiritually? Is there so much dust on your prayer life that it looks drab and dust-colored? Are there a few unwashed places in your life that are starting to smell just a little? Are there habits and favorite sins with so many little nooks and crannies that you've given up trying to change or clean them up? Has it been so long since the last spring-cleaning that you forgot what a fresh clean life is like? If the answer to any of these questions is yes, then let me recommend the best cleaning service I have ever found. He has great references. Here are a couple: 2 Corinthians 5:17, "Therefore if any man be in Christ, he is a new creature: old things are passed away; behold, all things are become new."; 1 John 1:9 "If we confess our sins, he is faithful and just to forgive us our sins, and to cleanse us from all unrighteousness."

So, if you are like most of us, it may be time for a little house cleaning. Go ahead, contact the best spiritual cleaning service in the universe, roll up your sleeves and follow His instructions. And, while you're at it, do some actual dusting at home. Happy cleaning!

COMMON SENSE APPLICATION

1. Remind yourself who Jesus is and what He wants to do in your life by rereading the gospels, Matthew through John.

2. Become active in a Christian group of Single Adults who are spiritually serious about life. If one doesn't exist, start one.

3. Try the web for resources and ideas at:
www.singlesmall.com or
www.singleadultministry.com

TO WASH OR NOT WASH

You might be a single man if ...
you divide your laundry into two piles;
dirty you have to wash and dirty you can wear again!

While serving with the Army in Germany, I worked with a lot of young helicopter pilots, most of whom were single. The discussions in the Pilot's Ready Room often centered on issues affecting single men. There was one particular single guy who always looked as though he had just crawled out of bed, you know, with wrinkled clothes and ragged appearance. One day the conversation centered on the "L" word; laundry. He said how much he hated doing laundry and that he had decided he just wasn't going to do it. It became clearer to us why his personal hygiene had become an issue among the other pilots. He related how he had decided to spend extra money on clothes and then wear them as long as possible. In his apartment he had selected the second bedroom floor as a clothes hamper and just threw all dirty clothes in there! That way, he only had to wash (or pay someone else to do it) when the atmosphere became unacceptable, about once every few months. I remember one time when he threw away a three-month collection of dirty underwear and bought all new ones!

I know that sounds disgusting but don't we do the same thing with unconfessed sin? It's a lot like unwashed laundry; after awhile everyone around you can begin to tell. The longer you allow laundry or unconfessed sin to build up in your life the more difficult it is to commit to addressing the problem. Somehow, you start learning to live with it and at some point you just don't notice it anymore. God notices but He never sees so much that He can't or won't forgive. 1 John 1:9 says, "If we confess our sins, he is faithful and just to forgive us our sins, and to cleanse us from all unrighteousness." God leaves the first step to us, the admission that our sin is a problem and our confession. He then keeps His promise and ". . . though your sins be as scarlet, they shall be as white as snow;" Isaiah 1:18. Remember 2 Corinthians 5:17, "Therefore if any man be in Christ, he is a new creature: old things are passed away; behold, all things are become new."

COMMON SENSE APPLICATION

1. Develop the habit of immediate confession. Wherever you are, driving (don't close your eyes!), at work, in class, on a date, wherever, obey the direction given in 1 Thessalonians 5:17, "Pray without ceasing."

2. Find a Christian friend to be your accountability partner/prayer partner. Call him when you find yourself drifting into a buildup of unconfessed sin. Ask him to pray with and for you.

3. As far as laundry goes, find the proper settings on your machine for "light" loads and wash often or go to the laundromat often. Some people actually use their washing machine as a laundry hamper! Be careful, though, about mixing whites and colors in the same load, unless you like the rainbow look!

PERSONAL NOTES

THAT EMPTY FEELING

*There's a God-shaped hole in every person.
Only Jesus can fill it!*

One day a little boy accompanied his mother to the super market and as they entered the large foyer there were the typical children's games and toys to keep the kids busy. The boy ran over to the electric horse and got in line with the others, waiting his turn. Beside the horse was a set of pay scales where one could put in a quarter and receive the "bad news" in front of everyone around. A huge man stepped upon the scales and put in his quarter, not noticing the Out Of Order sign taped to the side of the scales. As the little boy watched, the indicator on the scales started up and stopped at 50 pounds. With wide eyes the boy looked at his mother and said, "Look, mom, a hollow man!"

As I look at Christians today, both married and single, I see a lot of hollow people. To be honest, there are times when I feel a little hollow myself. That feeling usually hits me when several things are true: I fail to maintain a special time alone with God; my prayer life falters; I get too busy to worship; or when other things take priority over spiritual things in my life. I talk and counsel with a lot of Single People, mostly Christians, who are trying to fill hollow places in their lives. They sometimes try filling those places with things that don't satisfy for very long. Have you ever been to a circus or state fair? Remember the cotton candy? They give you a huge portion of that fluffy stuff and when you start eating it you notice that it immediately disappears in your mouth; there is very little substance there. Once I took the whole serving of Cotton Candy I bought and wadded it up the size of a golf ball! It is never as filling as it looks initially!

I have discovered that in order to really get filled up you have to choose carefully the things you consume. Ephesians 5:18 says,

"And be not drunk with wine, wherein is excess; but be filled with the Spirit." It is amazing how the Spirit can be more filling than any physical thing you include in your life. If you really want to know what being satisfied is all about, ask God to fill you with His Spirit and begin to fill your life with more substance than you ever imagined.

COMMON SENSE APPLICATION

1. Step One of being filled with the Spirit is to accept Jesus Christ as your Savior. Reread the salvation scriptures to ensure you understand the process God established by which we become Christians. I like the Roman Road; Romans 3:23, 6:23, 5:8, 10:9-10 and 13, and I John 5:11-13. If you've never truly accepted Jesus as Savior and you seriously want a right relationship with God, do so right now. Pray to Him; confess your sins and ask for forgiveness, ask Jesus to come into your heart and be your Savior, thank Him for saving you and then ask Him to help you make Him Lord, controller, of your life.

2. Step Two is to change the priorities you have for your time; include more scripture and prayer in your life. Make time each day to get alone with God so He can impress His will upon you.

3. Step Three is to fill your life with quality Christian friendships in a group or atmosphere where Christian values and principles are the primary focus.

HOW DEEP IS YOUR WATER?

It's just no fun in the shallow water!

Have you ever been to the lake? I have. If you're like me you hate the shallow water along the shore! Shallow water is no fun at all; you can't swim in it, you can't water ski in it, you can't fish very well in it, you can't go boating in it, you can't...well, you get the point. All you get in the shallow water is that yucky green stuff between your toes, your feet get tangled in the debris discarded by others, you step on whatever has washed up to the shore and you sometimes get cut by broken bottles and cans thrown there. Deep water, on the other hand, is a lot of fun! You can do all the things that you can't do in shallow water. However, there are risks in deep water too. You need help to survive for very long; you need things like boats, life preservers, swimming lessons, and friends who are good swimmers.

I see a lot of people these days, single people included, who spend most of their time wading around in shallow spiritual water. Sadly enough, they rarely experience the fun of being totally immersed in the spiritual atmosphere that God has for them. Some ask me, "Why isn't God blessing me with success (or relationships, or recovery, etc.?"). When I ask about their prayer life they have little to say. When I ask about the time they spend in the Bible they admit that it is very little. When I ask where they were for weekly Bible Study or Worship they make excuses. When I ask what ministries they are committed to they look confused. When I ask about their social lifestyle they don't want to talk about it. I heard someone say that the good news is that Christianity is nationwide but the bad news is that it is only one inch deep. I am amazed at how many people fail to see a connection between who they are spiritually and the blessings they want in their lives. You see, God doesn't just want a commitment of our resources; He wants US! When you read about tithing in the Bible you will soon understand that the tithe includes our time, our commitment, our willingness and our effort. Malachi wrote about the results of tithing in Malachi 3:10, "Bring ye all the tithes into the storehouse, that there may be meat in mine house, and prove me now herewith, saith the LORD of hosts, if I will not open you the windows of heaven, and pour you out a blessing, that there shall not be room enough to receive it."

COMMON SENSE APPLICATION

1. Make a list of the ways you currently commit your time, effort and resources to God.

2. Evaluate your success in each of these areas by determining the spiritual growth you experience or the value you add to the lives of others.

3. Pray for wisdom and courage to make positive changes in your commitment to God.

4. Be realistic; don't make promises you know you can't keep. Make changes in your life one step at a time.

PERSONAL NOTES

BURN BABY, BURN

Stay out of the sun if you don't want to get burned!

When I was a kid, our Little League baseball team celebrated the season's end by going to a local lake for a day of fun which included grilling burgers, swimming, boating and water-skiing. It was my first actual trip to a lake for recreation purposes and my first attempt at water skiing. I spent virtually all day in the sun with no shirt. Several adults mentioned that I was looking a little pink and should maybe put lotion on or wear my shirt. But the cool water and breeze had me convinced that I would be OK and that the adults were just trying to spoil my fun. That was the worst sunburn of my life! I was out of action for several days, not to mention the pain.

Years later, on a Mission trip to Mexico, we had a down day at the beach. I warned several young adults who were obviously getting too much exposure to the sun. Most didn't listen and spent 10 very painful hours in the van the next day before we got home. Likewise, we are in for a lot of pain when we get lulled into believing that exposure to sin and compromises in our lives will not burn us. Protect yourself. When Satan tried to burn Jesus through temptation, Jesus commanded Satan to get behind Him. In Luke 4:8 these words are recorded, "And Jesus answered and said unto him, Get thee behind me, Satan: for it is written, Thou shalt worship the Lord thy God, and him only shalt thou serve."

In Acts 1:8 Jesus said, "But ye shall receive power, after that the Holy Ghost is come upon you: and ye shall be witnesses unto me both in Jerusalem, and in all Judaea, and in Samaria, and unto the uttermost part of the earth." Jesus gives you the power to decide what will be in your life. Use the power wisely!

COMMON SENSE APPLICATION

1. Write down those people, places and things that end up burning you spiritually. Ask God to help you defeat the temptations, then put action in your prayers by separating yourself from those temptations.

2. Write down those people, places and things that help and encourage you in your walk with God. Take steps to put more of them in your schedule and lifestyle.

3. Oh, by the way, the most wide-spread cancer in America is skin cancer. So, it is best to avoid the sun as much as possible. When you will be in the sun with skin exposed for any length of time be sure to use sunscreen with an SPF rating of at least 15. You will be glad you did! Whatever you do, don't put butter on a sunburn; that's an 'old tale' with no foundation in fact!

PERSONAL NOTES

SHARPEN YOUR AXE

*Sometimes, even doing the right things
will cause you to lose your edge.*

I heard a story recently about a young man who wanted a job as a logger. As the story goes he asked the foreman of a logging crew for a job. The foreman said, "First, let me see you take this big tree down." In only a short while the young man skillfully felled the great tree. The foreman was impressed and said he could start on the next Monday.

Monday, Tuesday, and Wednesday went by. On Thursday the foreman approached the young men and said, "you can pick up your pay on the way out today." "But wait a minute" the young man said, "I thought you paid on Fridays." "Normally we do," said the foreman, "but we're letting you go today because you've fallen behind. Our daily charts show that you've dropped from first place on Monday to last place on Wednesday." "But I'm a good worker," the young men objected. "I arrive first, leave last, and I've even worked through my coffee breaks." The Foreman thought for a minute and asked, "Have you sharpened your ax?" The young man replied, "No sir, I've been working too hard to take the time."

Have you fallen behind in life because you failed to maintain a sharpness that allowed you to succeed? Has your relationship with God faltered because you failed to keep your relationship sharp with prayer and Bible study? Have relationships become shallow or ended completely because you failed to keep your personal relationship skills sharp? When was the last time you took time to learn something new in your career or in your relationship life or spiritually? The sit and soak principle may work for relaxing in the tub after a long day but if you stay too long, all you get is wrinkled! Eccl 10:10 says, "If the iron be blunt, and he do not whet the edge, then must he put to more strength: but wisdom is profitable to direct." In other words, if you allow yourself to become dull in life, especially in your spiritual relationship, more strength (effort) and skill (experience) will be required just to fulfill normal requirements. I encourage you to keep your ax sharp.

COMMON SENSE APPLICATION

1. Keep your career ax sharp by striving to be the best employee possible. Always be on time and put in extra effort for your employer. Look for and share creative ways to improve the productivity of your organization. Use education and experience to improve your job skills. Take advantage of every opportunity to increase your skill and knowledge about your career.

2. Keep your relationship ax sharp by making good relationship decisions. Work on the toughest relationship skill of all, communication. Read books that encourages and illustrate how to maintain quality in your relationships. If you are seriously considering marriage, DO NOT proceed without pre-marriage counseling. Get advice from your minister or a Christian counselor.

3. To keep your spiritual ax sharp be consistent in Bible Study, prayer, worship and Christian fellowship. Read 2 Timothy 2:15 and 2 Timothy 4:2. Caution: Avoid groups of Christians who talk a good line but spend most of their time and effort on worldly things.

THIN IS IN

But, be careful how thin you get!

I once heard a joke about a painter hired to repaint a church. After painting only one third of the front he realized he was running out of paint. With profit as the motive he thinned down the paint, then continued to paint the church. When two thirds complete he again realized that he had not thinned the paint enough so he thinned it a second time and completed the job. Up close all the paint looked the same but as the preacher drove up and viewed it from a distance there were obviously three distinct shades of paint on the church. Proud of his work the painter yelled to the preacher, "Well, what do you think?" The preacher pointed his finger at the painter and yelled, "Re-Paint, and thin no more!"

OK, so it was a lame joke but it proves my point. Thin is not always good. In the glitzy world of Hollywood and the media thin seems to win out over everything else. The thin fashion models displayed everywhere tell us we are not beautiful or handsome enough and that we all weigh too much to measure up. All too often though, thin is just an indicator of shallow, in both the Hollywood world and in the real world. There seems to be shallowness all around, in work ethics, in relationships, in families and in the spiritual commitments of people who call themselves Christian. In Luke 5:4 Jesus told Peter to go out in the deep water because He knew that was where the fish were. It is only when we get away from the thin and shallow that we experience the fullness of what life and God have to offer. Sure, there are always risks in these areas but risks can be healthy because they teach us discipline and help us appreciate what we accomplish in life. So, In a world of light this and that, reduced whatever and Readers' Digest condensed everything else, it is good to know that God has a FULL MEAL for those who are hungry for Him. Matthew 5:6 gives the menu. Jesus said, "Blessed are they which do hunger and thirst after righteousness: for they shall be filled." When it comes to God's best for us I don't want to be on a diet, I want to be filled to capacity. How about you?

COMMON SENSE APPLICATION

1. Look for indicators in your life that tell how thin or shallow your spiritual life is, things such as a lack of time spent with God in prayer or Bible study, lack of attention in spiritual situations, such as Worship Services, and so on.

2. Get into a serious Bible Study where God's Word is studied in depth and where there is openness to honest questions and discussion.

3. Search through your friends for a spiritual mentor who is deeper spiritually that you are. Ask that person to help you get to their level.

4. Remember, spiritually deep water can be as scary as actual deep water. Stick with your quest and make the commitment to grow deeper with God. II Timothy 2:15 says, "Do your best to present yourself to God as one approved, a workman who does not need to be ashamed and who correctly handles the word of truth."

ARE YOU FEELING CRABBY?

You must be in the basket!

John Maxwell is the founder of the INJOY Life Club, a leadership and mentoring organization I have used in my personal growth plan for years. He tells the story of a friend who was vacationing on the North East coast of the U.S. and was invited to go crabbing on the beach. He was handed a basket in which to carry the crabs as he picked them up off the sand. He asked his host how he was supposed to keep the crabs in the basket, since it had no top. The host said that a crab basket didn't need a top; it only needs two crabs. He went on to explain that crabs in the basket would not let any other crab climb out. As one tries to escape, the others will reach up and pull it back into the basket rather than help it get out. So, with two or more crabs you don't need a top; the selfishness of the crabs will do the job for you. But, that's the way crabs are!

I know some Single Adults who are just like the crabs. It seems that their mission in life is to ensure that others do not succeed. Usually, they have experienced some significant failure themselves and just can't seem to do what is necessary to recover and move forward. So, like the crabs in the basket, they make a point to discourage others, to pull them down to their level. I've even seen people pull their friends down spiritually, especially when their friend begins to grow deeper in God's Word and their life begins to be more of a reflection of Christ. People like that are spiritual crabs; they don't want anyone to grow above them.

The Old Testament warned about them, even back then. Deuteronomy 11:16 says, "Take heed to yourselves, that your heart be not deceived, and ye turn aside (*from God*), and serve other gods, and worship them." In the New Testament Paul cautions against them in I Corinthians 10:12, "So, if you think you are standing firm, be careful that you don't fall!" (NIV) In

Hebrews 2:1 you'll find these words, "Therefore we ought to give the more earnest heed (*pay more attention*) to the things which we have heard, lest at any time we should let them slip." In a more modern setting Eleanor Roosevelt said, "No one can make you feel inferior without your permission." All of these warnings make two things clear; first, others will try to pull you down and second, the choice is yours, you can stay up spiritually of allow others to pull you down. I encourage you to do the daily work of maintaining a close relationship with God, regardless of what the world around you says or does.

COMMON SENSE APPLICATION

1. Revisit who you are spiritually. Write out your testimony, your spiritual experience that brought you into a living relationship with Jesus. Thank God for that relationship.

2. Rehearse how you will respond to others who may tempt you to lower your spiritual standards by going places, doing things or making decisions that contradict your standards.

3. Make a personal commitment to put people and circumstances in your life that build you up rather than tear you down.

4. Make a commitment to find ways to lift up those who would try pull you down. But, be careful. If you start to waiver, abandon that effort!

JUST A STONE'S THROW AWAY

David had the first rock group!

You know the story of the classic confrontation between David, a young single, and Goliath, recorded in the Old Testament in 1 Samuel Chapter 17. If not, go read it and then come back to this page. Anyway, we are all proud of the way 'Little David' trusted God and defeated the 'Big Giant' with just a sling and a small rock. We may even have this image of little 'weak' David, twirling that sling, maybe with his eyes closed, waiting for God to direct the stone to the right spot. Maybe it happened that way, but when I study David's life before the giant I see him differently.

Chapter 16 records Saul's search for someone to play soothing music for him. As a young Single Adult David must have already had a reputation for excellence because of what Chapter 16, verse 18 says, "Then answered one of the servants, and said, Behold, I have seen a son of Jesse the Bethlehemite, that is cunning in playing, and a mighty valiant man, and a man of war, and prudent in matters, and a comely person, and the LORD is with him." So, David already had a reputation for bravery and he was experience in battle. Now look at Chapter 17, verses 34-38; David killed a lion and a bear to protect the family sheep. I can visualize David, out with the sheep, bored to tears, passing the time by practicing with his sling. I'll bet he became a 'pro' at hitting all kinds of practice targets and then finally the vicious animals which attacked the sheep.

The point is this. David was not some little wimpy kid; he was a prepared ready instrument that God could use to work His will for His people. Certainly God can use anyone He chooses to represent him but when you examine the scriptures you'll see that God most often used those who were serious in their relationships with Him and who had done the work to prepare themselves for service. It's possible but I doubt that God is going to 'zap' you with sudden spiritual depth or increased commitment to Him. It is through the small successes that He grows you into the 'warrior' you need to be for him. Like David, you must be willing to do the small things and be willing to take risks that build your spiritual character into what God wants. Remember, giants will always come, masked as challenges or failures. Be like David; he discovered that overcoming challenges was just a stones throw away!

COMMON SENSE APPLICATION

1. On separate cards, write down at least three of the major challenges you are facing right now. On each card list the things that must happen for you to overcome that challenge, leaving space to record when each thing is accomplished. Put the cards in a prominent place where you will see them often

2. Make a list of the changes you need to make in your life to create an atmosphere for learning and growth; habits you must kick, disciplines you must embrace, commitments you must make, etc.

3. Share your lists with a trusted friend who will commit to pray for you to redirect your life. Be sure to celebrate with Christian friends when God helps you overcome these challenges.

FIRST FLIGHT

Dreams can soar on wooden wings.

Have you ever been accused of 'day dreaming?' I've been a dreamer since I was a child. As an eight year old on our small East Texas farm I used to dream of flying. I now hold a commercial pilot's license for airplanes and helicopters and I remember vividly the flight test that qualified me as a commercial pilot. But, that was not my first flight. I remember, we lived directly under the flight path of Air Force B-52 Bombers, which trained in North Texas, and we saw many airplanes flying over. I used to watch those big airplanes and wonder what it would be like to be the pilot, far above the earth, soaring through the clouds. My dream was to someday be a pilot.

One Saturday 4 of my brothers and I had a free afternoon and were playing in the barn. There were some old boards lying around, so they decided to build an airplane. They nailed two boards in the shape of a cross and nailed a smaller one across the main board near the back, thus completing the fuselage and front and back wings. They put a vertical fin on the back and made a cockpit from an old apple crate. One of them cut a piece of tin in the shape of a propeller, twisted it so it would be turned by the wind and nailed it on the very front. A big stick appeared from somewhere and was nailed to the floor inside the apple crate, to provide controls. The airplane would not compete with any of the major aircraft manufacturers but it was complete.

I was the youngest and lightest one there so they all decided I was to be the pilot. My older brother Jack placed me in the cockpit and spaced the three oldest ones around the plane, one on each wingtip and one in the back. They lifted the little wooden airplane up onto their shoulders and ran out of the barnyard and toward the back fence. I was gripping that stick tightly and the wind was turning the tin propeller. Then, something amazing happened; I pulled back on that stick as I had done so many times in my dreams. And, in my eight-year-old mind, that airplane lifted off the shoulders of my brothers and cleared the fence! I could see myself climbing over the pond near the barn, crossing the stream and turning over the cornfield as I circled and climbed toward the clouds. I could see my brothers far below in the back yard, waving to me as I climbed into the clouds to join in a flight of Air Force airplanes. That was my first flight. And, I can truthfully tell you this, that flight was as real to me as the one that got me the Commercial License!

It's all about being able to dream about the future and take steps necessary to bring your dreams into reality. Proverbs 29:18 says, "Where there is no vision the people perish." (KJV) When you are in tune with what God wants for your life the vision will become more clear and in agreement with Jeremiah 29:11, "For I know the plans I have for you, declares the Lord, plans to prosper you and not to harm you, plans to give you a hope and a future." (NIV)

COMMON SENSE APPLICATION

1. Take some 3X5 cards and write a dream of yours on each card, as many as it takes. Place these cards around in different rooms where you will see them often.

2. As you concentrate on each dream begin to jot down on that card your plan for making that dream come true. Record when you complete each step toward that dream.

3. Stick to your plan until you begin to see more of your dreams really come true.

YOU CAN'T JUST SIT THERE

Be ready to tie helium balloons to your lawn chair!

I read an old news report recently in the Internet files of the Los Angles Times covering an event that took place in July of 1982. A 33-year-old single truck driver named Larry Walters was arrested for an unusual flight he took over the city (http://www.markbarry.com/amazing/lawnchairman.html). It seems that Larry had always dreamed of flying and had even joined the Air Force to pursue his dream. However, his eyesight disqualified him. Years later, at 33, he again pursued his dream in an unorthodox fashion. He purchased 45 large helium weather balloons from the Army/Navy store, tied them to an aluminum lawn chair, strapped on a parachute, took a CB Radio, some food and drink, took a pellet gun to pop some balloons so he could come down. Some friends then cut the tether holding the chair to his car bumper!

Larry thought he would float just above his neighborhood. He was shocked however when his over-inflated lawn chair shot up to 16,000 feet into the approach course to the Los Angles International Airport! Both Delta and TWA pilots sighted him as they came out of the clouds, sitting there in his lawn chair! Can you imagine those flight crews trying to explain a flying lawn chair to the Airport Radar Controllers? Larry drifted out over the ocean and then back over land and finally popped out a few balloons so he could descend. Just as he was landing, the tether lines got caught on the high voltage lines near Long Beach, CA., sending the city into a 20 minute blackout!

As Larry was arrested a reporter asked him, "Why do you do it?" Larry said a profound thing. He said, "A man can't just sit there!" Truth be known, there are untold numbers of Single Adults who are just sitting there; not pursuing the God-given dream inside of them. Many are trapped inside walls that they built themselves.

Maybe you are one of them. If you are a Christian Single Adult you need to remember that dream pursuing begins with the first step, found in Proverbs 16:3, "Commit thy works unto the LORD, and thy thoughts shall be established." I encourage you to stop sitting there and use the steps below to pursue your dreams.

COMMON SENSE APPLICATION

1. Write down that dream you have always had but have not seriously pursued. It may seem wild and crazy when you see it in writing but write it anyway. Your dream may be a career or a place or financial success or have to do with family or relationships. Write it down. Now get serious by analyzing your list and narrowing your focus. Eliminate the whims on your list and zero in on your true dream.

2. Share your dream with trusted friends and others, maybe older and wiser, whom you respect. Don't be reluctant to get advice and allow others to hold you accountable as you make your plans. Proverbs 15:22 says, "Without counsel purposes are disappointed: but in the multitude of counsellors they are established."

3. Write down every action you must do to make your dream come true. Maybe you need to get out of debt. Maybe you need to get more education or stop a habit. For each action, list the things that must be accomplished. Leave a blank to check when you accomplish each of them.

4. Don't be like most people, satisfied to just sit there! Pursue your dream! Psalm 20:4 says, "May he give you the desire of your heart and make all your plans succeed." (NIV)

LEARNER'S PERMIT

A piece of paper doesn't prove that you are ready for marriage!

I've read different reports and heard other seminar speakers talk about the high per-centage of Single Adults who have as a major goal to be happily married. Some say as high as 95%. I don't know the exact number but I am sure that a majority of the Single Adults I know would fall into the want to be married category. In my nine years plus at my current church there have been over 180 weddings! Regardless of the previous marital status of those getting married I see an almost universal belief that love will conquer all and that they don't need to worry about learning to communicate or how to negotiate differences or how to set marital goals. Most believe that marital bliss will just happen!

Other than an eternal relationship with God, the most critical thing that people do is the thing for which they get the least amount of training and take the least amount of advice. That is, marriage! If you want to be a plumber, an engineer, a surveyor or a doctor you must go through months or years of training, spend lots of money and take difficult tests to get your certification. Even for a driver's license, teenagers have to get a Learner's Permit and practice for months before they can get a real license. For marriage you just have to spend a few dollars, go through a 15-minute ceremony, say 'I do' and you are married! In Genesis 2:24 says, "Therefore shall a man leave his father and his mother, and shall cleave unto his wife: and they shall be one flesh." The reason it is so strange is that when this appeared in the Bible, there were no mothers and fathers, only Adam and Eve! God set a high priority on marriage when He pulled it up from history and put it in with the creation process.

We require extensive premarital counseling at our church before couples tie the knot. I encourage all couples to view their Marriage License as a Learner's Permit. All Single Adults need to understand that putting two imperfect people, male and female, together with the goal of being married forever will require a lot of WORK and a lot of learning! The first thing they have to learn is the true dimension of love. Jesus said in John 13:34 "A new commandment I give unto you, That ye love one another; as I have loved you, that ye also love one another." How did Jesus love us? In Matthew 20:28 it says, "Even as the Son of man came not to be ministered unto, but to minister, and to give his life a ransom for many." So, the first task in a marriage is to SERVE your mate; to give your life for them if necessary. That's a pretty tall order! I'd say that level of commitment requires some serious soul-searching before saying 'I Do.' To serve someone else we have to overcome the biggest barrier to marital success, our own selfishness. It destroys our ability to communicate on a deep level. Communication is the only tool we have to build true emotional, mental and physical intimacy in marriage. Intimacy is the thing that glues us together forever. Love is a great foundation but there are times when, humanly speaking, you don't deserve to be loved. That's why it is WORK, the work of learning and growing together, that makes marriage last forever.

COMMON SENSE APPLICATION

1. Read, "Finding The Love of Your Life," by Neal Clark Warren. ISBN 1-56179-008-5 Published by Focus on the Family. It is a little technical but the principles are practical and effective as you pursue that permanent relationship.

2. Take plenty of TIME; experts say 2 years from meeting to marriage.

3. If you are divorced, go through a Recovery seminar before forming a serious relationship.

4. DO NOT get married without going through Christian based Pre-Marriage Counseling.

LOOK BEFORE YOU LEAP

Don't go off half-cocked!

Have you ever heard the old saying, "Don't go off half-cocked?" Growing up on a farm we did a lot of hunting. That way we put a lot of meat on the table for our family of 10. I remember that our shotguns had a *safety*, activated by pulling the hammer half way back, into the *half-cocked* position. That way we could walk safely through the woods toward the hunting area. Once in the hunting area we were supposed to pull the hammer all the way back to be ready to fire. I was too young to have a gun but I remember some of my brothers failing to bring home supper because they left their guns in the half-cocked position and couldn't fire when the opportunity arose.

I'm talking about being prepared for whatever endeavor you are pursuing. Luke 14:28-30 says, "For which of you, intending to build a tower, sitteth not down first, and counteth the cost, whether he have sufficient to finish it? Lest haply, after he hath laid the foundation, and is not able to finish it, all that behold it begin to mock him, Saying, This man began to build, and was not able to finish." I see a lot of Single Adults who waste too much time and energy starting or getting involved in things without considering the full impact on their lives. This mistake takes a wide variety of forms. I see a lot of Single People, especially young adults, who make significant financial commitments based on a *whim* or on poor research and end up over their heads in debt, especially credit card debt. Some will make the decision to change jobs so often that they never build a foundation in a career and do not have the experience or training to move to a higher level in salary or any other area of concern. There are many who do not *consider the cost* of too quickly moving through the preliminaries of a relationship into a serious commitment, only to be hurt as the relationship falls apart. Or, worse yet, to get married and constantly struggle trying to negotiate their differences or end up a statistic in the divorce records.

I realize that we live in a microwave world. We get impatient if our meal takes more than three minutes to prepare. However, when you compare a microwave dinner to a 5-course meal carefully prepared at a fine restaurant I think you would choose to wait patiently. We get *suckered in* to being impatient because most things in life seem to happen quickly. TV sitcoms show people meeting and ending in a *happily ever after* embrace in 30 minutes. Divorced people are told to *get over it* and *find somebody new*! Advertisers tell us we can *have it all* and we can also *have it NOW!* It is okay to rush some things but when considering the things that really matter it is best to listen to the truth in Galatians 5:22-23, "But the fruit of the Spirit is love, joy, peace, longsuffering (*patience*), gentleness, goodness, faith, meekness, temperance (*self-control*): against such there is no law. How about that; **patience** is a spiritual thing that will help you in the real world and can prevent you from going off half-cocked!

COMMON SENSE APPLICATION

1. In financial matters, delay commitments for a period of time and consult trusted advisors. Go to a *Dave Ramsey* Financial Peace Seminar if possible
(www.financialpeace.com).

2. In relationship matters, be *slow* to commit your heart and very careful to analyze the impact on your life.

3. In spiritual matters immerse yourself in God's Word on a daily basis. Find a church with quality Bible Study and Worship and attend regularly. Develop a consistent prayer life.

WHAT'S IN A WORD?

I know you thought that what I said was what you thought I said, but what you thought was not what I meant.

We live in a very confusing world. We seem to be most confused by the details of our relationships with others. We humans are most challenged in our interpersonal communications. The main problem is the different meaning we place on the words we use. As a pilot I like the illustration of the depressed copilot. The pilot had been trying to cheer him up prior to takeoff without success. During the takeoff roll he looked over at the copilot and said, "Come on, cheer up!" Amid the noise of the engines the copilot thought he said, "Gear up," so he lifted the switch to the UP position. They both watched helplessly as the airplane settled on its belly in the middle of the runway!

Your miscommunications may not cause an airplane wreck but I have seen relationships and friendships wrecked by misunderstandings. If it weren't for all those confusing words we'd all communicate better! You know those words; love, commitment, truth, etc. Our human traits make it even more difficult. H. Norman Wright, in his pre-marriage book, *So, You're Getting Married?* reports that only 7% of effective communication happens through hearing. Over 70% comes from visual signals such as body language, surroundings, etc. Yet our society continues to find more ways to communicate without personal contact. The written word has been around forever. E-mail is the latest edition. I am writing this at the moment, in a coffee shop at the Kansas City Airport. I've been processing the e-mail in my Palm pilot. I know, I know, I am part of the problem too! But, a few minutes ago a man named Michael asked to share this table. He asked what I do for a living. I talked about Single Adult Ministry and the issues involved, including divorce recovery. I saw his countenance change and his eyes sadden as he shared about his recent divorce and asked for my advice. He and his wife were both Christians but still made poor choices en route to marital failure. They had stopped communicating and couldn't understand each other. SEEING him and HEARING him helped me to better understand and recommend an appropriate action. In this case e-mail would have been inadequate to help Michael.

Many people misunderstood Jesus. Even the disciples didn't always 'get it.' In Matthew 13 Jesus told the parable of the sower. The disciples got him aside, and asked for an explanation. In verse 9 he had said, "Who hath ears to hear, let him hear." Most everybody has ears! But, I think he meant, "Those who are willing to shut out the world and concentrate on what is important, they will be able to hear the truth." He went on to say in verse 16 that they were blessed because they wanted to see and hear the truth he was sharing.

COMMON SENSE APPLICATION

1. Remember, personal contact is always the best way to communicate. When matters get serious, stay away from e-mail and chat rooms. Rather, meet with the person!

2. When communicating in person, be sure to look the other person in the eye and work hard at actively listening. God gave us two ears but only one mouth; there must be a lesson there!

3. Don't be afraid to ask questions and repeat important information to make sure you understand what the other person is saying.

4. Be clear and honest in your own communications with others, especially in your communications with God. He will always listen and understand.

DOES SOMETHING SMELL FUNNY TO YOU?

*Could it be the black kitty
with the white stripe down his back?*

I know God must have made skunks for a good reason. Not being a *skunk-lover* I just can't quite fathom what that reason could be! I remember the day on the farm when my Dad and one of my brothers *treed* a skunk, thinking it was a opossum. The skunk won the confrontation and they were left in the middle of the stream trying to wash the smell off so Mom would let them in the house! One minister of Music I served with built a large beautiful house on a golf course soon after he arrived in town. There was one flaw, a gap in the access door leading under the house. Months later, during mating season for skunks, a half dozen of the creatures chose the crawl space of his house for their romantic encounter. The humans upstairs knew something wasn't quite right but thought it was just wisps of skunk-dom from the fields nearby. It wasn't until the skunks chewed a hole in the duct work to the air conditioning system that the full effect of the unwanted guests was realized. At that point the situation was untenable and required immediate action. Hundreds of dollars and one *skunk-trapper* later the skunks were finally on their way to a new home.

Sometimes in life Single Adults will leave *gaps* in their spiritual lives. Before long, unwanted temptations and influences sneak in and occupy space intended for better things. Soon, things begin to smell funny! You begin to notice that there is something unpleasant about your life and your relationship with God. When you fail to notice *gaps* in your life and fail to keep out the things that don't belong you can end up in sin. It doesn't take much sin to make your life begin to smell. Ecclesiastes 10:1 says, "As dead flies give perfume a bad smell, so a little folly outweighs wisdom and honor" (NIV). I'm not the sharpest knife in the drawer but I'm smart enough to know that *wisdom and honor* are always better than a *skunk* under the house! I advise you to choose wisdom and honor.

COMMON SENSE APPLICATION

1. When you let sin creep in slowly it is not always obvious at first. That's why you need a trusted Christian friend who has a good sense of spiritual smell and who will agree to be your accountability partner. Give that friend permission to be honest and up-front with you about areas of your life that are showing gaps. Listen and take action to keep your life smelling sweet.

2. Be consistent in your attendance at worship services and in Bible Study. Guard your mind to keep it focused on the Word.

3. Keep the cobwebs off of your prayer life. It may help to keep a journal of prayer concerns and records of answered prayer.

4. If you consistently find that there are gaps in your spiritual life it may help to go to the zoo, take a picture of a skunk and tape it to your mirror! Every morning you will be reminded what it *smells like* to God when you allow sin into your life.

PERSONAL NOTES

WHAT GOES UP, MUST COME DOWN

What do you do in an airplane when the engine quits?
Obey the law!

Being a pilot I know the answer to the classic question; what do you do if the engine quits? Answer: Obey the law of gravity! In 1642 Sir Isaac Newton defined the Law of Gravity, which states, "All objects in the universe attract each other with a force which is proportional to their masses and inversely proportional to the square of the distance between their centers" (http://csep10.phys.utk.edu/astr161/lect/history/newtongrav.html). Sounds pretty complicated to me! All I know is, when I drop something it always falls to the floor and usually rolls under the lowest piece of furniture and ends up against the wall with the dust and spider webs! You know what I'm talking about. Here's the point; things that are dropped always end up lower than they were before.

Let's look at it another way. Things that are not kept up will invariably do down. For instance, if you don't keep the maintenance up on your car, it will deteriorate in its usefulness as a vehicle. If you don't keep up with your car keys you just might be late to work. If you don't keep up with the latest changes in your career you will be left behind. If you don't keep up with what it takes to maintain a relationship it will become shallow and could fail. If you don't keep up with your need for spiritual growth you will become spiritually dry and be a better target for Satan. Get the point? It takes a lot of effort to keep things up! Left to themselves most things will deteriorate, go down, fall, fade, etc.

Paul warned what would happen if you do not keep up with learning spiritual principles in an environment with Christian friends. In Colossians 2:8 he warned, "Beware lest any man spoil you through philosophy and vain deceit, after the tradition of men, after the rudiments of the world, and not after Christ." Those who are not up on their spiritual philosophy are more susceptible to the false philosophy of others. Paul also said, in I Corinthians 16:13, "Watch ye, stand fast in the faith, quit you like men, be strong." When you stand firm in your faith it will not so easily deteriorate or go down.

COMMON SENSE APPLICATION

1. How do you stay up spiritually? I guess I could say that this devotional is brought to you by the letter 'D'; discipline! First it requires a genuine desire to stay up. Remind yourself of the benefits of an up relationship with God. Think about how your heart is at peace when you and God are in close relationship. Commit yourself to a consistent routine of Bible study and prayer.

2. Develop a credible accountability partnership with a trusted friend who will tell you when you are slipping downward in your spiritual excellence and help you re-energize your close walk with God.

3. Reduce the distractions in your life that tend to encourage sloppiness in your spiritual life; things such as inappropriate TV programs, discouraging music, frequenting inappropriate places and even friends who do not care about spiritual excellence.

4. Get ready for some spiritual sweat because it takes WORK to stay UP

DON'T LET THE FIRE GO OUT

Beware of Christians who are on constant standby to put out your spiritual fire before it gets to them.

When my mom and dad were a young couple they were farmers living along the northeast Texas side of the Red River, separating Oklahoma from Texas. The name *Red* came from the red color of the water, caused as it washed away the red Texas clay along the riverbank. The Red River was prone to flooding and often changed course as the riverbank eroded. Over the years the river had gotten closer to their small farmhouse due to erosion. Whenever the river flooded and the riverbank began to slowly crumble into the water my dad would build a small bonfire within a few yards of the edge. During the night he would get up often to make sure the fire was still burning, which would indicate that the river had not gotten closer to the house and washed away the ground under the fire. My dad knew that the only time he really had to worry was when the fire went out.

Have you ever felt like the foundation under you has begun to erode, to crumble away? Has your *fire* for life, for your job and for spiritual things started to dim? Maybe it has even gone out! If so, you're not alone. I see Single Adults often who have given up on life. A major part of my ministry with Single Adults centers on *encouraging* and *rebuilding*. I want Single People to see that God has given them the tools necessary to become happy productive *on fire* Christians. All they have to do is apply these tools. I Corinthians 12:4-6 tells that there are different tools, or *gifts*, that we have as Christians, "Now there are diversities of gifts, but the same Spirit. And there are differences of administrations, but the same Lord. And there are diversities of operations, but it is the same God which worketh all in all."

Young Single Adults need to realize that landing that first career and the first significant relationship will take *time*! Single adults who are recovering from loses in relationships need to remember that healing and redirection take *TIME*! If you are struggling in any area of your life it could be that you are not properly tending your spiritual fire. You should consider a trip out to gather some more firewood!

COMMON SENSE APPLICATION

1. Add *fuel* to your spiritual fire by being an active participant in a local Single Adult ministry or spiritually based group. Spend more *time* in God's Word; try II Timothy 2:15 as an encouragement.

2. Add *air* to your fire by breathing a prayer daily as you spend time with God.

3. *Fan* your fire by taking enthusiastic action on the principles God has set down for your life. Colossians 3:23 says, "And whatsoever ye do, do it heartily, as to the Lord, and not unto men."

PERSONAL NOTES

FINISH WHAT YOU START

*Success begins by taking the first step.
Failure is certain if you don't take the second step.*

I grew up in a large farm family: mom and dad, seven boys and three girls. Our farm was a small one tucked back in thick, piney woods in the northeast corner of Texas. One particular year we saw Daniel Boone on our black and white TV and got inspired to build a log cabin. With all those pine trees it should have been easy. We attacked a grove of pine saplings with our saws and axes and began to assemble the cabin. At about the one-foot height it occurred to us that we didn't have a clue how to leave space for the door and windows and still keep the thing together. So, we abandoned it, went to a new spot and started another one, hoping to discover the secret to doors and windows as we went. Today, if the elements had spared the logs, you could see eight or ten unfinished log cabins in those woods, all without doors or windows!

Do you have trouble finishing what you start; in your relationships, in your career or in your service to the Lord? In my counseling and while traveling to Single Adult conferences around the country I meet many Single People who are frustrated with their inability to accomplish what they consider to be significant things for themselves. Sometimes things don't go as planned in several areas of our lives and it is difficult to keep motivated to do what is required to see it through to the conclusion. Does that sound like you? You're not alone; a lot of people feel that way from time to time.

We can learn a lot from the apostle Paul, a single adult, as he writes to Timothy, another single adult. In 2 Timothy 4:7-8 he said, "I have fought a good fight, I have finished my course, I have kept the faith: Henceforth there is laid up for me a crown of righteousness, which the Lord, the righteous judge, shall give to me at that day: and not to me only, but unto all them also that love his appearing." I pray that you won't quit when things get tough, especially in your relationship with God! All relationships take a lot of work. Our relationship with God is no different. Commit yourself to do the work of becoming more of what God wants you to be and to finish what you start.

COMMON SENSE APPLICATION

1. If you have trouble finishing personal or professional projects, start by breaking the project into segments which can be completed one at a time. Set time deadlines for each and force yourself to stick to the time allotted. Get a mentor or accountability partner who can encourage or chastise you as needed to ensure accomplishment of your goals.

2. If you have trouble in your commitments to God you need to set aside more time to spend in His Word and in prayer. Involve yourself deeper in the life of your church or Christian group and seek another Christian you trust to help guide and encourage you. The Christian life is not easy, just worth it!

PERSONAL NOTES

TRADITION KILLS

We've never done it that way before!

A Navy pilot and I were sharing stories we had experienced in his Naval Aviation career and my Army Aviation career. He told me about a fellow pilot who had flown the same type of jet aircraft for years and had actually ejected from a disabled airplane several times by pulling the ejection lever located on either side of his pilot's seat. The Navy retired the old planes and taught him to fly a new more capable one but he constantly talked about how he wished he still had the old plane. The new plane was faster, had better weapons and had an improved ejection system with a handle in front of the seat and one overhead, giving the pilot a better chance to reach the handle regardless of the airplane's position.

One day the pilot was landing the new plane on an aircraft carrier when the landing cable that grabs the hook on the plane to stop it, broke and allowed the jet to continue down the deck and plunge off the front of the aircraft carrier. When the controller saw the cable break he radioed the pilot to EJECT, EJECT, EJECT! The pilot never ejected. Rescuers pulled the wreckage out of the ocean with the pilot still in the cockpit; he had drowned. When they took the body out, a crewman noticed that the ejection handles had not been pulled, but the seat had been bent upwards on both sides, right where the ejection handles had been on the old airplane he loved so much. An unwillingness to change had led to the pilot's inability to make the right choice in an emergency.

Are you stuck in a rut? As a single person, how do you react when you sense that God wants you to break out of your mold and do a *new thing* for Him? Maybe He wants you to change a routine that has prevented you from being available to your group for a ministry that you've never done before. You must be willing to take risks and embrace the unknown if you are going to get out of your comfort zone for God. Isaiah 43:18-19 says, "Forget the former things; do not dwell on the past. See, I am doing a *new thing*! Now it springs up; do you not perceive it? I am making a way in the desert and streams in the wasteland."

COMMON SENSE APPLICATION

1. Go to your Single Adult leader or pastor and ask for help in discovering your spiritual gifts. There are several good tests available. I recommend the spiritual gifts assessment and the accompanying personality assessment provided in the single adult personal empowerment book, *Start A Revolution*, by Stephen Felts - ISBN 0-8054-9823-0 published by LifeWay Press.

2. Make a list of the habits (traditions) in your life which limit your availability to fully serve the Lord. Be honest now! Make a commitment to start changing them, at least one at a time. I have heard that, with concentrated effort, you can change a habit completely in 31 days. Why not start today?

3. Volunteer to be part of an existing ministry team that is making a *real* difference in peoples lives. Better yet, you organize a ministry team to meet an identified need in lives. Caution: Don't let yourself get on a ministry team that is just a *social group* or one that does not have a real ministry to accomplish. We don't need more *holy huddles*, we need ministers!

SOMETIMES YOU JUST CAN'T WIN

Is there ever a good time for things to go wrong?

Did you ever notice how things seem to break down or blow a fuse at the worst possible time? The water heater goes out on Friday night instead of Monday morning. You run out of hot water at the beginning of your shower rather than at the end. The electricity goes off just as you turn on the hair dryer. The car breaks down on the way to work instead of after work. And, well, you get the point! Life can be full of annoyances, for both single women and men.

Sometimes though, life can hit you with real challenges. Your relationship falls apart. Your boss blows a fuse. Your family suffers a tragedy. Most of you have been there. It seems as though no one is going through what we have to endure. We often wonder if anybody knows or cares how we feel. Jesus does!

Jesus was no stranger to annoyances or real challenges. He told His followers to expect to put up with the things of this world because they were not of this world (John 17:16) In John 16:33 Jesus said, "In the world ye shall have tribulation: but be of good cheer; I have overcome the world."

COMMON SENSE APPLICATION

1. For electrical outages keep a few large candles in each main room of your home. Make sure you have matches to light them.

2. If the water goes off, remember, there are gallons of fresh water in each toilet tank, not toilet bowl! It is not usable for personal hygiene purposes, however, if you use any additive such as drop-in chemical cleaners or those that color the water. Don't EVER use it for drinking or cooking!

3. If the heat goes off, close off all but one room by closing doors and blocking the space under the door. Your body heat and any appliances still-working will produce enough heat to warm the room a little. It's a good idea to buy a small electric heater if you have recurring heat system problems. Provide ventilation and do not close off the room if you use kerosene or other fuel type heaters!

4. To keep the general annoyances and even serious events of life in perspective read about the life and ministry of Jesus in the four gospels (Matthew, Mark, Luke and John) and the challenges the apostles faced in the book of Acts.

PERSONAL NOTES

SEPTEMBER 11th

Our world will never be the same.

Who will ever forget where they were and what they were doing on the morning of September 11, 2001, when terrorists onboard 4 high-jacked airliners slammed into the World Trade Center, the Pentagon and a Pennsylvania field? Since the 2002 Census shows that about 75 million adults in America are single (www.census.gov) it is a forgone conclusion that many on the airplanes, in the buildings and members of the rescuers who died were single people. Some who made peace with God or shared God with others in the final moments were single. Many who ran into the burning buildings as others ran out were single. Many who dug with their bare hands at Ground Zero, and still dig as I write this, are single. And most in the military units who were sent to take the War On Terror to the enemy's front door are single. My son who lives in Queens near Ground Zero is 28 and single.

September 11th brought home the reality that life is fragile and short, that evil is real and the human spirit is resilient. The acts of courage and sacrifice committed by people, many of them single, will be remembered throughout our lifetime. Ezra 10:4 says, "Rise up; this matter is in your hands. We will support you, so take courage and do it." There were many people that day that took courage and helped save lives.

In most tragedies throughout history single people were involved in making a positive impact on the world. David, the young single sheepherder, made a giant contribution in the defeat of the enemies of Israel. As revealed in Acts 17:6 the Apostle Paul, a single, met a big challenge and 'turned the world upside down.' And of course, the ultimate Single Adult, Jesus Christ, taught us how to respond to tough times when He said in John 16:33, "I have told you these things, so that in me you may have peace. In this world you will have trouble. But take heart! I have overcome the world."

September 11th changed the world. How did it change you? Do you appreciate freedom more now? Do you have a fresh appreciation for fire fighters, police officers and our military? As a Christian do you have a new urgency to share Christ with those around you? All of us will have to come to terms with this unspeakable tragedy. Those who know Christ as Savior have the assurance that Paul was right in Romans 8:38-39 when he said, "For I am persuaded, that neither death, nor life, nor angels, nor principalities, nor powers, nor things present, nor things to come, Nor height, nor depth, nor any other creature, shall be able to separate us from the love of God, which is in Christ Jesus our Lord."

COMMON SENSE APPLICATION

1. To really appreciate the freedom afforded by America, reread the history of our country. Plan a vacation to Washington D.C. to visit our country's roots.

2. Take time to tell the fire fighters, police officers and military personnel in your community that you appreciate their commitment and service.

3. Recommit yourself to spiritual excellence. Attend church and Bible Study regularly. Write down and rehearse a 1 minute and 3 minute version of your salvation testimony and pray for opportunities to share it with those in your world. You never know when it might be their last chance to meet the Christ who can secure their future in Heaven.

PERSONAL NOTES

PERSONAL NOTES

PERSONAL NOTES

PERSONAL NOTES